Sewtastic!

PaRragon

Bath · New York · Singapore · Hong Kong · Cologne · Delhi
Melbourne · Amsterdam · Johannesburg · Shenzhen

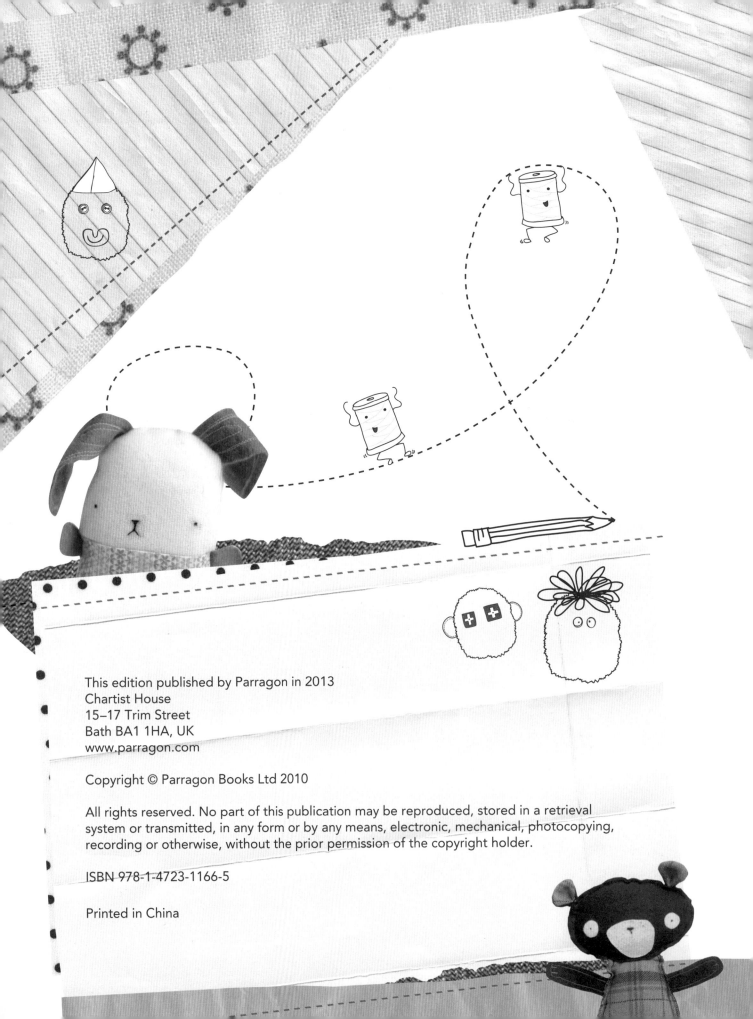

This edition published by Parragon in 2013
Chartist House
15–17 Trim Street
Bath BA1 1HA, UK
www.parragon.com

ISBN 978-1-4723-1166-5

Printed in China

Contents

About this book

Are you GIRLIE? A ROCK CHICK? Into QUIRKY AND TOTALLY INDIVIDUAL STYLE?

Take the makes in this book and let your imagination run wild.

There are NO limits

The crafts and instructions are specific enough to help out a beginner, but they've got enough variety to please the pickiest of pros. Whatever your level, this book gives you the skills and guidance you need to make your own things.

The best part about the makes is that they're totally eco friendly and low cost. All you have to do is reduce, reuse and recycle – and raid your wardrobe! Use clothes you've grown out of, stray buttons, ratty blankets, even old curtains...

JUST DON'T FORGET TO ASK YOUR PARENTS FIRST!

HELLO

TOOLS & TECHNIQUES

5

SEWING KIT

You really don't need too many materials to get started. Most things you'll find around your house. If you need a bag to keep everything in, why not make it yourself? Check out the next section!

Every sewing kit should have:

Needles
A mix of needles is best: use medium-length, sharp needles for general sewing, and shorter quilting needles for the really finicky work. Needles with long eyes are for embroidery.

Cotton sewing thread
A whole load of different colours is a must for the modern sewer. You normally want to match the colour of the thread to the fabric, but sometimes you want it to stand out, so pick boring colours, such as black and white, and bold colours, like purple, too!

Embroidery thread
Embroidery thread is much thicker than sewing thread and is used to decorate rather than attach fabric together.

Pins

You'll need pins to hold fabric in place while you lay it out and start sewing. Store your pins in a cool pincushion that you make yourself!

Scissors

Use a small pair of scissors for cutting curves and clipping thread, and a large pair for cutting big pieces of fabric and big shapes. Check with an adult about these.

Ruler

For measuring lengths of your materials.

Glue

It's best to find some craft glue that you know will work on different types of fabric.

Buttons

Never throw a stray button away! You never know when a lonely little button will be the perfect finishing touch to your make. Keep your buttons in a cool container.

Ribbon

Don't get rid of any ribbon either! Keep a collection of it — short pieces, long spools of it... and then you'll always have a way to glam up your makes.

FABRICS

When you're sewing, remember that every fabric is different.

FELT

Felt is the easiest material to handle. Even if you're just starting out, you (yes, you!) can handle it. Felt is easy to cut and doesn't fray. Remember that felt doesn't like to be bathed and might act up if you try to put it in water!

COTTON

If you're going to use cotton (like an old shirt), wash it first. That way it won't shrink if you wash it after you make it into something new, and your new item will smell nice and fresh (and not like an old shirt)!

FLEECE

An old fleece is a great material for making a new scarf, but just remember that fleece is a bit stretchier than cotton and felt, so be careful not to pull on it when you're cutting and sewing.

LEATHER

If you're lucky enough to be allowed to use an old piece of thin leather, be extra careful and maybe even use a thimble while you're stitching. Leather is really tough and needles don't like to go through it very easily.

STUFFING

You'll need to stuff most of these super-cute makes to add the cuddly and squishable factor. There are loads of different stuffing materials you can use.

Try these ideas:

Cotton or polyester filling

This is the traditional stuffing and can be bought at a range of shops. If you get a high-quality filler, you'll get a professional-looking make. No lumps or anything!

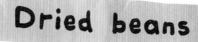

Dried beans

This is another popular choice and gives a different feel. This is good for juggling balls, door stops and makes where you want a beanie feel.

Dried rice

Here's another popular option, similar to dried beans. And you probably already have some at home! Just ask your parents if you can use it first.

Potpourri

See if you can track down some scented filling like dried lavender. A softie stuffed with a scented filling makes an awesome gift!

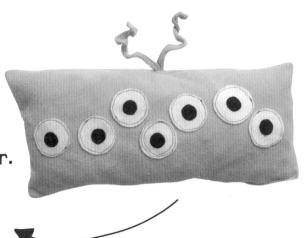

You can even try socks, wool, tissues or newspaper if you want to use what you've got lying around at home. This won't feel as professional as cotton filling, but it will make each softie unique!

When you stitch up the hole you've used to stuff your softie, try this trick to make the hole invisible:

Fold the fabric inside, tuck it in neatly and use tiny stitches to close the hole. The rough edges will be secretly hidden!

11

SOME stitches

Running stitch

Running stitch is the most basic of stitches. You simply bring your needle up through your fabric at point A and down again at point B to make a little line of thread. If you keep doing this in a straight line, going in and out of the fabric, you can sew a basic seam and stitch fabric together.

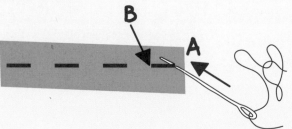

Backstitch

Backstitching is taking the running stitch to the next level. Start at point B, bringing your needle up through the fabric, and stitch back down through point A. Then bring your needle under the fabric, past point B, come up at point C and then down again at point D. Because you're going over the stitches, this is a super-solid way to stitch two pieces of fabric together.

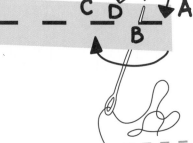

Satin stitch

Use the running stitch, but do a whole bunch side by side to make a shiny, satiny row of stitches.

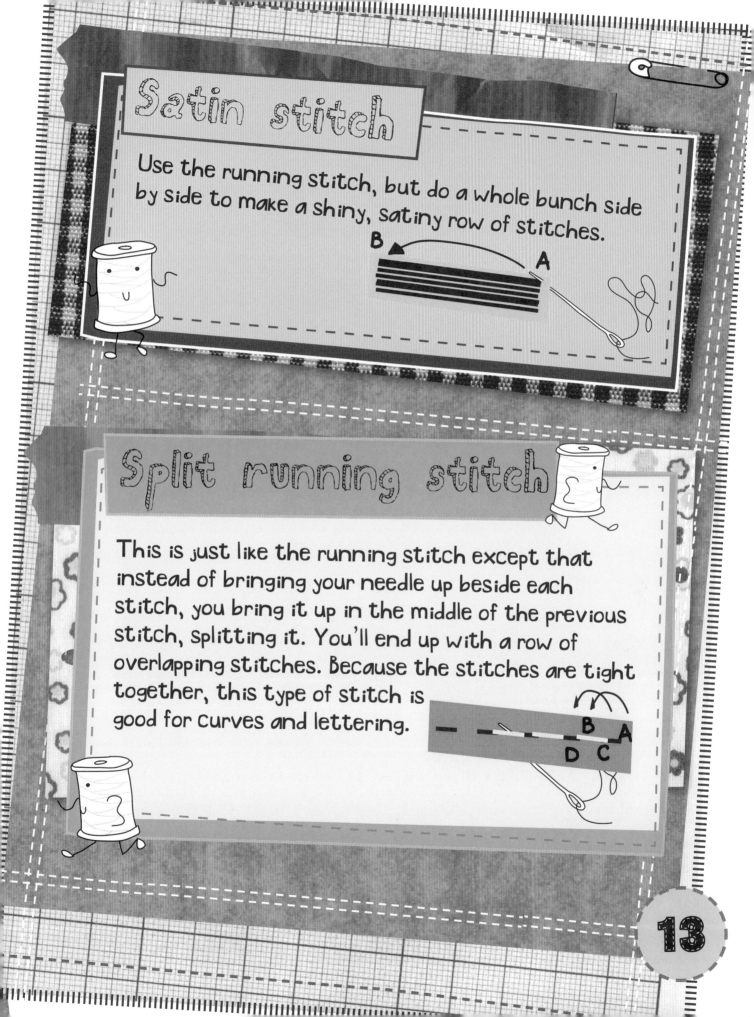

Split running stitch

This is just like the running stitch except that instead of bringing your needle up beside each stitch, you bring it up in the middle of the previous stitch, splitting it. You'll end up with a row of overlapping stitches. Because the stitches are tight together, this type of stitch is good for curves and lettering.

START TO STITCH

You're probably thinking, all this sounds so awesome and I can't wait to get started... but how DO I start?

- Firstly, get your needle and thread ready.
- Cut a piece of thread about an arm's length.
- Then thread your needle (get the thin little piece of thread through the tiny hole in the needle).

Have patience! You can do it!

- Once the thread is through the hole, move the needle to the middle of the thread and fold the thread in half. Having a double layer of thread will keep your stitches super strong.
- Lastly, tie the two ends together with a knot near the end of the thread. You may need to tie a few knots on top of each other so the thread doesn't slip through your fabric.

Finishing stitching

OK, so you know how to get started, but once you start, how do you stop? You can't just leave your needle hanging there! To finish up, do a few stitches on top of each other to secure the thread, or, if you want the end to look super tidy, stitch through the thread on the underside of the fabric a few times so no one but you will know the extra stitches are there.

When you're happy that your stitches aren't going anywhere, snip the thread close to the fabric – but not so close that it comes right out! Then your needle is finally free.

Wait, there's one more thing!

Sewing on a button!

1. Thread your needle with some thread that matches the colour of the button.

2. Lay the button in place on the fabric.

3. From under the fabric, push the needle through the fabric and up through one of the holes of the button.

4. Pull the thread all the way up, until the knot is tight against the fabric.

5. Next – you can probably guess! – is to go back down through another hole in the button, and straight down through the fabric.

6. Repeat this three more times to secure the button in place. If the button has four holes, do this three times diagonally one way, and three times diagonally in the other two holes.

7. When you've finished make sure your needle is under the fabric. Thread it through the thread under the fabric and tie a double knot.

And that's it!

HOW TO APPLIQUÉ

What does appliqué mean, anyway? It's simple, really. We're cutting out shapes of one fabric and sticking them to another. This T-shirt is done this way.

We're going to use adhesive web to do the sticking.

I was done with appliqué!

Your final picture is going to be a mirror image of the template you use. It gets flipped over, so if you're doing letters, remember to draw them backwards!

How to appliqué

1. Trace one of the templates at the back of the book or draw your own onto the side of the adhesive web.

2. Cut roughly around the edges of the shape. This is your chance to be messy – it doesn't have to be perfect yet!

3. Place the shape adhesive side down on the fabric you're using for the shape. Ask an adult to iron it in place. If you're using patterned fabric, make sure you stick the paper to the non-patterned side.

4. No more Mr Messy Guy! Cut carefully around the edges of your shape. This time you're cutting the paper and the fabric since they are stuck together.

Fabric

Template

5. Peel the backing paper off the shape and turn it over. The side with the adhesive on it will be rough, and the other side will be untouched, so you'll know which is which if you get confused.

6. Place the shape on the side of a bag, the front of a pair of jeans or the back of a tee. Ask an adult to iron it in place with a cool iron. Press the iron down instead of sliding it on the material so the shape doesn't move around.

7. Lift the iron and check out your awesome appliqué. Ta-da! That shape should be stuck on good!

COSY EGG COSiES

Keep your boiled eggs cosy with these super-cute egg warmers.

To make the penguin, YOU'LL NEED:

- 2 pieces of black felt, about 9.5cm at the base
- 2 white felt circles
- 1 small triangle of orange felt for the beak
- 2 buttons
- Patterned fabric for his belly, about 6cm at the base
- 2 pieces of black felt for the wings
- White and black cotton thread and glue

HERE'S WHAT YOU DO:

 Stitch or glue the white felt circles to one piece of black felt, and stitch the buttons on.

 Glue on the beak.

 Glue or stitch on the patterned belly fabric.

 18

4. Place the penguin face down on the other piece of black felt.

Base layer

Top layer

Wings in between

5. Place the wings between the fabric. Stitch around the penguin sides and top, but don't touch the bottom.

6. Turn right side out.

Use the same process to make an edgy egg warmer. Try a badge and patterned fabric instead of felt and cute penguin features.

19

POM-POM FUN

Pom-poms are adorable little mates.

HERE'S WHAT YOU DO:

1. Use a compass to draw a circle about 5cm across on the cardboard, and cut out. From the centre of the circle, draw another smaller circle, 2cm across, and cut this out. Repeat to make one more ring.

2. Put the two pieces of cardboard together to get one sturdy donut.

3. Wind the wool around the donut. Work your way around until all the card is well covered.

4. Ask an adult to help you cut all the way around the outer edge of the donut, snipping the wool as you go.

5. Slide a piece of wool between the two pieces of cardboard and wrap it around the donut. Pull tight to tie all the pieces of yarn together. Then remove the cardboard.

20

6. Fluff up the pom-pom and trim it to make it nice and neat. Glue on the eyes and ribbon!

HAIRBAND

Floppy annoying fringes will be a thing of the past with this make! And even if you don't have a fringe to hold back, a hairband can be a cool accessory for any style!

YOU'LL NEED:

- 2 pieces of patterned or plain fabric, about 40cm x 6cm
- A piece of elastic, 15cm long

HERE'S WHAT YOU DO:

1. Put your two pieces of fabric together (patterns facing in).

2. Use chalk or a pencil to mark a line 6cm in from each end.

3. Sew inside the marks along each long edge using a running stitch.

4. Turn right side out.

5. Slide your elastic inside one of the open ends. Push it up to where the stitches end and pin in place.

← Elastic

6. Repeat step 5 with the other end of the elastic and the other hairband opening.

7.

Secure the elastic at each end by doing a running and back stitch across each line.

23

USING DENIM

Do you have jeans with holes in the knees or that are too short for you now? Don't throw them out! You can get a whole new wardrobe item out of them!

ALERT! ALERT! Ask an adult to help when you're cutting and sewing denim.

MAKE DENIM SHORTS OR A SKIRT

Turn your jeans into shorts or a skirt and no one will ever know they nearly went into the bin. You can do this with other trousers too.

HERE'S WHAT YOU DO:

 Ask an adult to iron the jeans so you're working with a like-new piece of fabric.

 Fold the legs on top of each other along the fly.

 Mark where you want the shorts or skirt to end, adding an extra inch for the hem. Use a ruler to draw a straight line from seam to seam on each leg. Make sure this line is under the pockets and crotch.

4. Cut along each line. You'll now have a pair of shorts! All you need to do now is turn the insides of the legs inwards about 2cm and use a nice thick needle to stitch the hem.

5. To make a skirt, you need to use a needle or scissors to take out the stitches that make the crotch. Do this a few stitches at a time. Ask an adult to help you.

6. Pin the left and right front pieces of the denim (the pieces that used to be the crotch) one over the other and stitch them together. Do the same for the back pieces.

7. Turn the bottom of the skirt up about 2cm towards the inside. Ask an adult to press it down, and then sew around it to make a nice clean hem.

transformation

MOTIF TEE

Just hanging out for a bit...

To make this super-cute T-shirt you'll need:

- Brown felt fabric cut to the shape of a bear (use the template at the back of this book)
- White felt fabric cut to the shape of a bear, but bigger than the brown felt version
- White fabric for the eyes and mouth
- Pink felt for the inner ears
- Embroidery thread
- Black cotton thread

HERE'S WHAT YOU DO:

1. Doing a running stitch with your embroidery thread, stitch the brown and white felt bear pieces together.

2. Glue the pink bits to complete the inner ears.

3. In the centre of each white piece of eye felt, do some small running stitches very close together with the black cotton thread.

Running stitch

4. On the white piece of mouth felt, use a satin stitch with the black cotton thread to make a nose and mouth.

Satin stitch

TIP: Use a pencil to draw a faint line for the nose and mouth before stitching.

5. Glue the eye and mouth pieces of felt to the brown bear face.

6. Glue or appliqué the face to the front of your T-shirt.

LET IT DRY THEN WEAR THAT BEAR!

SQUARE CUSHION COVER

This cushion is simple yet makes a serious splash on your sofa. First, find a plain cushion that needs a cover.

YOU'LL NEED:

Tweet

- 1 square piece of plain fabric, about 2cm longer on each side than your cushion
- 1 square piece of patterned fabric, the same size as the plain fabric square
- Fabric, buttons, felt, ribbons – anything to make your cushion stand out!
- Velcro, the length of one side of the plain fabric square
- Black and white cotton thread

HERE'S WHAT YOU DO:

1. Stitch, glue or appliqué your design onto the plain fabric square.

GLUE

Velcro strip

2. Turn the design face down and stitch one of the Velcro strips along the bottom of the square.

28

3. Turn the patterned fabric face down and stitch the other part of the Velcro along one edge.

4. Place the design face down against the patterned fabric square (pattern facing the design).

> Make sure the Velcro pieces are lined up!

5. Stitch along the two sides and the top of the cushion using the backstitch, leaving the Velcro edges open.

6. Turn the cover right side out. Then pop the cushion in and keep it secure by sticking the Velcro together.

LONG ALIEN CUSHION

This extraterrestrial cushion will bring extraordinary attention to your sofa or bed!

YOU'LL NEED:

- 2 pieces of fabric, about 60cm x 30cm. Fleece works well!
- 7 white felt circles, for the eyes
- 7 small black felt circles, for the pupils
- 2 pieces of fabric or felt, 16cm x 4cm, for the antennae
- 2 pieces of thin wire, each 16cm long
- White and black cotton thread and glue
- Stuffing

TO MAKE THE EYES:

For a cool alien effect, do a running stitch around each white circle with black cotton thread, and then glue the black pupil to the middle of each eye.

TO MAKE THE ANTENNAE:

Fold one thin piece of fabric in half with the wire inside and stitch all the way around using a running stitch. Do the same for the other antenna.

Folded in half

Wire inside

Put the two pieces of fabric together (outsides facing in), and stitch around the outside using the backstitch, leaving a small gap. Turn right side out and stuff, then sew up the small hole using the split running stitch.

Glue all seven eyes on. Sew the bottom of each antenna to the top of the cushion's back and then twist them for the final touch.

Hey human, I'm watching you!

TINY TOADSTOOL PINCUSHION

Have you ever seen such an adorable place to keep your pins? Super cute!

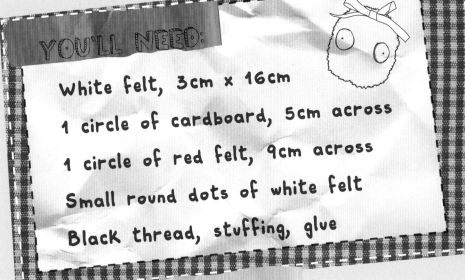

YOU'LL NEED:

White felt, 3cm x 16cm

1 circle of cardboard, 5cm across

1 circle of red felt, 9cm across

Small round dots of white felt

Black thread, stuffing, glue

HERE'S WHAT YOU DO:

 Starting at a short edge, roll the white felt into a cylinder. Draw on the eyes and mouth.

 Unroll the felt and stitch the face on with black thread.

 Now roll the felt up again and glue the end in place.

4. Place the red felt flat on a table. Pop a bit of stuffing in the middle and then place the cardboard on top.

Cardboard

Stuffing

Red Felt

 5. Do a loose running stitch around the edge of the red felt circle, pulling as you go so the middle gap is being closed over the stuffing and cardboard.

6. When you're done there should be a small hole under the cap of the toadstool. Wedge the white roll just inside this and glue in place.

Glue the white dots to the top of the toadstool.

Allow to dry then pin away!

33

ARM WARMERS

Are your arms always getting cold? Then they need some arm warmers to warm them up! And if you're not a cold-armed person... well, arm warmers make an awesome fashion statement, too.

YOU'LL NEED:

An old pair of long socks (wash them first!)
Cotton thread

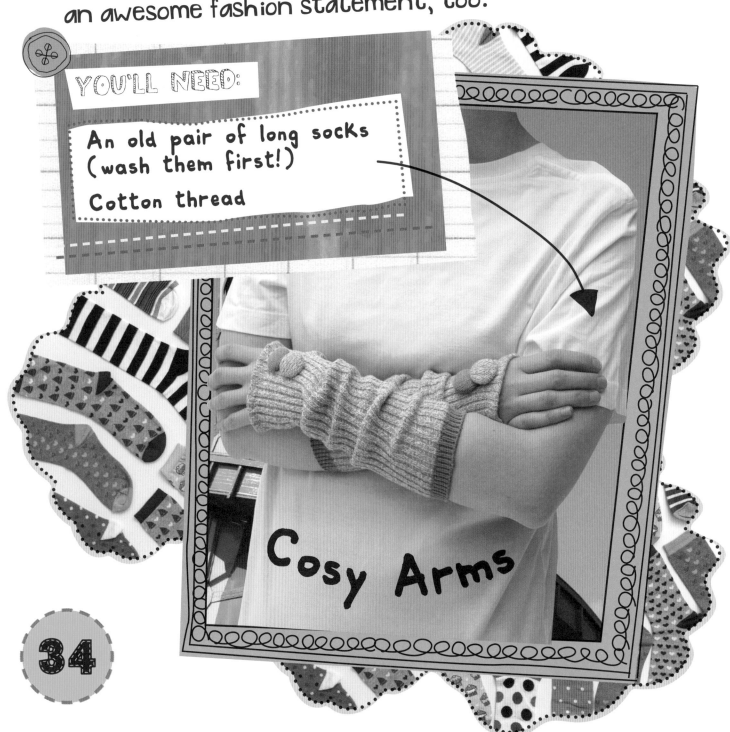

Cosy Arms

1. Pop your hands inside each sock and pull them right up to your elbows. Use a pen to draw a faint diagonal line where your thumb starts and another line across your knuckles (on the sock, not on your hand!).

2. Take your hands out and cut along the lines you've drawn.

3. Turn the socks inside out.

4. Fold down the seams of each hole you've cut about 0.5cm and stitch around the holes using a running stitch. You'll do a full circle to stitch the fold down. But be careful! Make sure you don't stitch up the hole by accident.

5. Turn the socks the right way out again.

TIP:
Try covering buttons with the cut-out pieces of sock and stitch these onto your new arm warmers.

SHOPPER BAG

YOU'LL NEED:

- Scissors, needle and thread
- 2 thin strips of plain fabric
- 1 large piece of strong plain fabric, 40cm x 56cm
- 1 smaller piece of patterned fabric, 28cm x 35cm

HERE'S WHAT YOU DO:

 1. Cut the plain fabric to measure 40cm x 56cm.

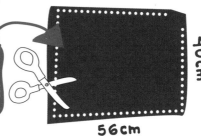

40cm

56cm

28 x 35cm

40cm

56cm

2. Cut the patterned fabric to 28cm x 35cm and stitch on top of the plain fabric with an equal gap at all sides.

Fold here

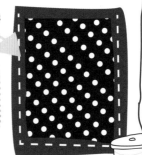

Warning! Don't sew up the top of your bag! Just sew along the white dotted line.

 3. Then fold the fabric in half along the long side, and stitch along the sides and bottom.

Use running stitch: it's quick & easy!

36

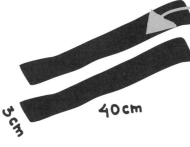

3cm   40cm

4. Cut two thin strips of the plain fabric to measure 3cm x 40cm.

Fold here

sew here

5. Fold the strips in half lengthways. Stitch all the way along the edges.

6. Make the strips into handles. Stitch one end inside the front panel of the bag, 4cm from the left edge. Then curl the strip round and stitch the other end 4cm from the right edge. Repeat this on the back panel of the bag with the other strip.

OUT and ABOUT

7. Adorn your bag with LOVELINESS! Try your fave pattern, like a skull and crossbones motif! AHOY ME HEARTY!

with my NEW BAG!

CLUTCH A CLUTCH!

YOU'LL NEED:

◎ Patterned fabric for the outside, roughly 37cm x 23cm.

◎ Bright piece of felt for the lining, also roughly 37cm x 23cm

◎ Small pieces of fabric, buttons or badges to decorate

◎ A fastener

◎ Coloured thread to complement the pattern of fabric you've chosen

Tweet

Tweet

Hello

HERE'S WHAT YOU DO:

1. Cut the patterned fabric and felt into 37cm x 23cm rectangles and lay the felt on top of the fabric.

37cm

23cm

Felt

Fabric

2. Use a straight running stitch to sew the felt and fabric together. Go all the way around the rectangle.

3. Fold the bottom of the rectangle about 15cm up, making sure that the patterned fabric faces out and the felt is on the inside.

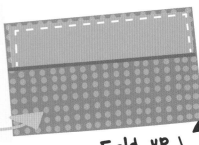

Fold up

38

4. Fold the top part of the rectangle down to make the flap of the clutch, and pin it carefully in place.

Fold down

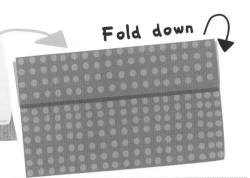

HELLO

5. Now – this is the fun part! – cut fabric in any shape you like, grab buttons or badges and start decorating! Place the pieces onto the clutch without attaching them.

TIP:
You can stitch letters onto your clutch using a split running stitch.

6. Once you're happy with your design, stick the pieces down with glue or, if you're super adventurous, try appliqué (see page 16).

Running stitch

7. Use a running stitch to stitch the bag together – but only go up to the flap on each side.

HELLO

8. Finally, stick your fastener to the inside of the bag, roughly in the middle, to keep your little clutch nicely shut while you're out and about.
Now you're ready to
SHOW IT OFF!

Hello

BUTTON BRACELET

For this make you'll need loads and loads of buttons and a long piece of elastic that's thin enough to fit through the button holes.

Thread the elastic through the button holes, pushing each button as far as you can to the end of the bracelet until you have a piece of elastic filled with buttons long enough to fit around your wrist.

Tie a knot tight against the last button to hold all the buttons securely in place.

Tie the two ends together.

Pop the bracelet on your wrist!

41

BUILD A BLANKET

THERE ARE LOADS OF DIFFERENT WAYS TO MAKE A QUILT OR BLANKET.

Try piecing more pieces of fabric together for a real patchwork feel for your quilt...

Or go with different PATTERNS and SHAPES to change up the style.

42

Instead of a decorative quilt, try a snuggly blanket made of fleece. If you haven't got an old fleece shirt as big as a blanket, you can buy a metre of fleece at a fabric shop for a low price. Fabric shops usually have plenty of different patterns to choose from, too.

When you've got your fleece, stitch shapes to it, or simply snip into one end, making 5cm cuts in every 2cm to get a fringed effect.

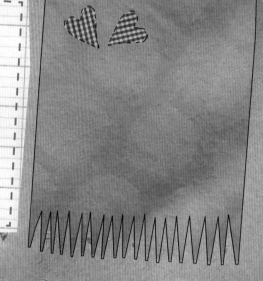

If you want a gift that leaves a lasting impression, a fleece like this is your ticket. It's simple and inexpensive, but such a thoughtful present.

PATCHWORK CHARLIE CHICK

This is another little guy who can stay small or be blown up nice and big. Use the template at the back of the book.

YOU'LL NEED:

- 2 pieces of white felt, cut to a chick shape
- 1 piece of red felt, cut to the shape of hair
- 2 pieces of red felt, cut to the shape of feet
- 1 piece of orange felt, cut to the shape of a beak
- Patterned fabric, about 5.5cm x 10cm
- Stuffing
- Black and white cotton thread

HERE'S WHAT YOU DO:

1. Stitch eyes to one piece of the white felt using the black cotton thread and a split stitch.

2. Stitch or glue the beak to the face.

3. Stitch the patterned fabric to the bottom half of the chick body front using the running stitch.

44

4. Place the chick face down on top of the second piece of felt chick body.

5. Pop the feet and hair in place between the two pieces of fabric.

6. Stitch all the way around, securing the feet and hair as you go and leaving a small hole at the side of the chick.

7. Turn the chick the right way out.

8. Stuff your chicklet with stuffing and stitch up the hole.

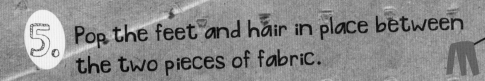

Chick face down

2nd piece of chick felt body

And here's Charlie!

Billy Bunny

Use the same instructions as for Charlie Chick but replace the beak with a little mouth and the hair with some bug bunny ears!

FELT TEDDY

This character is a bit more complicated to make, so let's break it down.

Use the template at the back of this book to get just the right bear shape!

To make the HEAD AND EARS, YOU'LL NEED:

- 2 circles of white felt for eyes
- 1 piece of white felt for the mouth
- 2 large pieces of brown felt, cut to the shape of a teddy head
- 2 pieces of patterned fabric, cut to the shape of ears
- 2 pieces of brown felt, cut to the shape of ears
- Black cotton thread
- Stuffing

MAKE THE EARS FIRST:

1. Place one piece of the patterned fabric and one piece of the brown ear felt back to back (pattern facing in).

2. Stitch all the way around the ear, leaving a small hole at the bottom.

3. Use the little hole to turn the ear right side out.

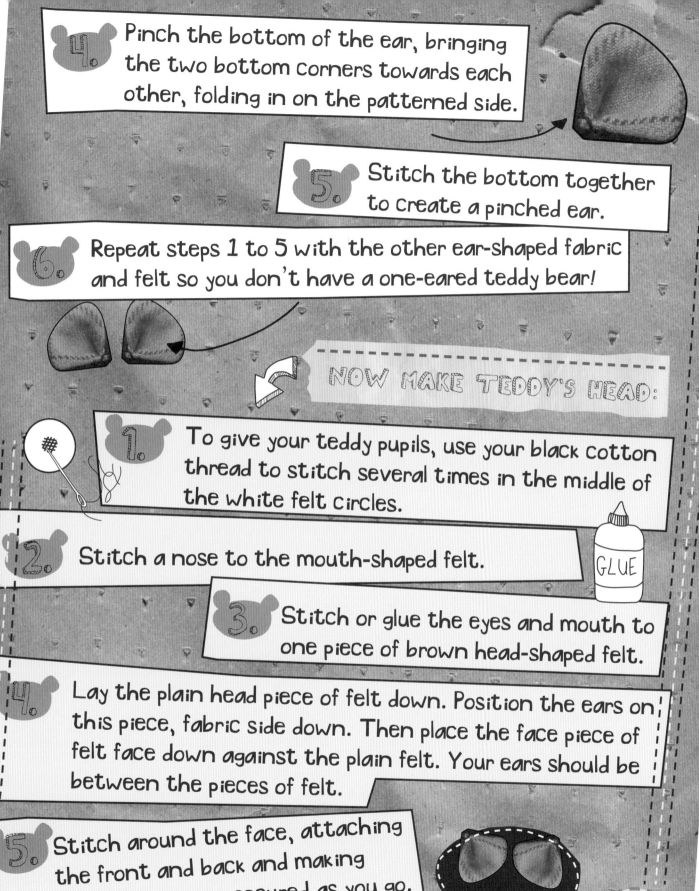

4. Pinch the bottom of the ear, bringing the two bottom corners towards each other, folding in on the patterned side.

5. Stitch the bottom together to create a pinched ear.

6. Repeat steps 1 to 5 with the other ear-shaped fabric and felt so you don't have a one-eared teddy bear!

NOW MAKE TEDDY'S HEAD:

1. To give your teddy pupils, use your black cotton thread to stitch several times in the middle of the white felt circles.

2. Stitch a nose to the mouth-shaped felt.

GLUE

3. Stitch or glue the eyes and mouth to one piece of brown head-shaped felt.

4. Lay the plain head piece of felt down. Position the ears on this piece, fabric side down. Then place the face piece of felt face down against the plain felt. Your ears should be between the pieces of felt.

5. Stitch around the face, attaching the front and back and making sure the ears are secured as you go. Leave a small hole at the bottom.

Make continues on next page

6. Turn the head the right side out and stuff the head with your stuffing.

To give your teddy a body, YOU'LL NEED:

 Patterned fabric (use the same as for the ears) cut to the shape of a bear body

- 4 felt strips, about 2cm x 6.5cm (for the arms and legs)
- 1 large brown piece of felt, cut to the shape of the bear's body
- Brown cotton thread
- Stuffing

NOW MAKE TEDDY'S BODY:

 1. Lay the brown felt body down and place the fabric pattern side down on top of it.

 2. Position the arms and legs in place, just in between the fabric and felt.

3. Start stitching at the bottom and work your way around the body, stopping a little before where you started to leave a small hole.

4. Turn the body right side out and stuff the body with stuffing.

 Now stitch it all together!

TEDDY IN A TREE

49

FELT DOLLY

To make a little dolly, use the exact same steps as for the teddy on pages 46 to 49, but use different colours of felt and different facial features to make this softie girlie rather than furry! Add stuffed arms and legs, too!

Attach the hair and clothes after you've put your doll together.

50

GIRLS JUST WANNA HAVE FUN!

51

MINI MASCOTS

Use the techniques on the previous pages to make yourself a teeny tiny softie. Make him out of felt or socks or whatever material you like best — the only difference from the earlier makes is that he's mini!

Very small but very CUTE

Be creative — go cute, quirky or COOL!

Take your mini mascot with you everywhere for good luck - and for fun!

He likes to hang off tote bags...

and hang out in the park...

careful he doesn't get lost out there!

Why not make your own template by drawing your own character to cut out.

53

SOCK MONSTER

To make this scary (but still super-cute) monster, **YOU'LL NEED:**

- 1 old sock (washed, please!)
- 1 small piece of felt, cut to the shape of a tooth
- 1 large button
- 1 covered button (wrap material around the button and fasten with glue or stitches at the back)
- Black ribbon, about 13cm long
- Black cotton thread
- Stuffing

HERE'S WHAT YOU DO:

1. Cut your sock across at the heel so you're only working with the flat foot bit.

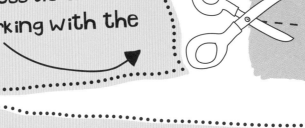

2. To give your monster eyes, stitch the two buttons to the sock.

3. To give your monster a mouth, use the running stitch to attach the ribbon to the sock.

4. Glue on the tooth.

5. Fill your monster with the stuffing, making him as chubby or skinny as you like.

6. Stitch up the opening of the sock so none of the monster's insides come oozing out.

GLUE

AAARRGHH! I AM THE SOCK MONSTER!

55

SOCK RABBIT

Step up your sock makes by taking them to the next level – this sock rabbit combines a sock with felt for an even more professional feel.

To make this super-cute rabbit, YOU'LL NEED:

- ◎ 1 sock
- ◎ 2 buttons
- ◎ Black cotton thread
- ◎ 1 circle of felt, 5.5cm across
- ◎ 2 pieces of fabric, cut to the shape of bunny ears
- ◎ Stuffing

HERE'S WHAT YOU DO:

1. Cut off the top (from the heel up) and bottom (from the toes down) of the sock.

Top

Bottom

2. Fit the circle of felt into the opening at the bottom of the sock, with the felt overlapping the sock by about 5mm.

3. Using the backstitch, sew all the way around the circle to attach the felt to the sock and close the bottom hole.

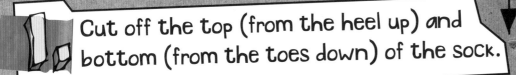

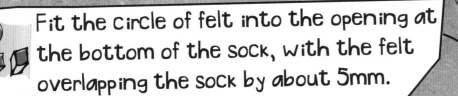

Felt

4. To give your bunny eyes, stitch the buttons to the sock.

5. To give your bunny a nose, stitch diagonally across several times.

6. Stuff your rabbit with cotton stuffing, beans or even tissues.

7. Pin the ears in place at the top of the rabbit, placing the ends just slightly inside the opening at the top of the sock.

8. Stitch across the opening using the backstitch to close the hole and attach the ears all in one go.

FABRIC FLOWER BADGE

This little blossom is a perfect touch to any outfit. Depending on the material you choose, it can be cutesy and girlie or edgy and cool... whatever your style may be.

YOU'LL NEED:

- Patterned fabric cut into 7 petal shapes
- Felt cut into 7 petal shapes (same size as the patterned fabric)
- A pretty button or badge
- Coloured cotton thread
- A safety pin

HERE'S WHAT YOU DO:

1. Place the patterned fabric petal and the felt petal together with the pattern facing inwards.

2. Stitch around the petal leaving a small gap.

3. Use the small gap to turn the petal the right way out.

4. Repeat steps 1 to 3 for the 6 other petals.

ALERT! Fiddly bit!

5. For a cool folded effect, pinch the bottom of a petal and sew through it, and then do this for all the other petals so you're threading through each of them and pinching them together as you go along. Go around several times to make sure your flower is secure.

6. Stitch a button to the middle of the flower.

7. Use a safety pin to attach the brooch to your clothes, scarf, bag or hat, or glue a proper pin brooch fastening to the back to be super professional — especially if this is a gift!

Flower Power

SPARKLY ROCK CHICK BADGE

Brooches were a must-have in the olden days, and they've come back in style big time. Make this sparkly rock chick badge to totally rock your outfit!

YOU'LL NEED:

A pin badge with a cool pattern
Sequins
6 ribbons, each about 8cm long
3 ribbons, each about 10cm long

TIP: Ribbons don't have to be actual ribbons. Try cutting straps from an old nightie or bag!

Cotton thread

HERE'S WHAT YOU DO:

1. Make each short piece of ribbon into a loop and glue the ends to the back of the badge to make this pattern.

GLUE

2. Glue as many sequins as you like to the three longer ribbons. Wait for them to dry.

3. Stitch the tops of the three sequined ribbons together.

4. Glue the sequined ribbons to the back of the badge.

TIP: Use a lot of glue and put something heavy on the ribbons so they dry securely in place.

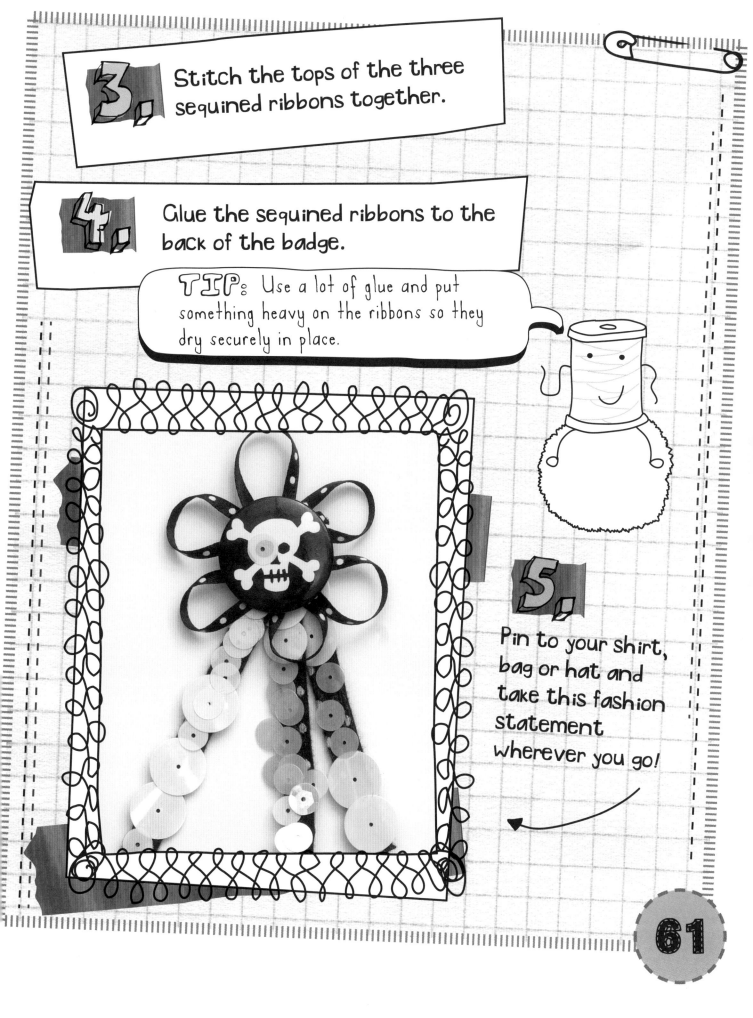

5. Pin to your shirt, bag or hat and take this fashion statement wherever you go!

SWEET DREAMS eye MASK

Do you or someone you know need a good night's sleep? Try out this super-sweet eye mask for sweet dreams and peaceful nights.

HERE'S WHAT YOU DO:

1. First, decorate the patterned fabric. This Night Night mask has words stitched on felt using a split running stitch, but you could try out buttons or ribbon or other felt shapes to adorn the mask with loveliness, too.

Try out quirky patterns too. How about a face on a face?

2. Next, lay the soft fabric on a table, soft side down. Then put the thick fabric on top of that and the patterned fabric on top of that, pattern facing up.

Patterned fabric

Thick fabric

Soft fabric

3. Position the ribbons on either side of the mask, with the ends tucked in the layers of fabric.

4. Stitch all the way around using the backstitch.

And that's it! A dark and good night's sleep is yours! Night night!

SWEET DREAMS...

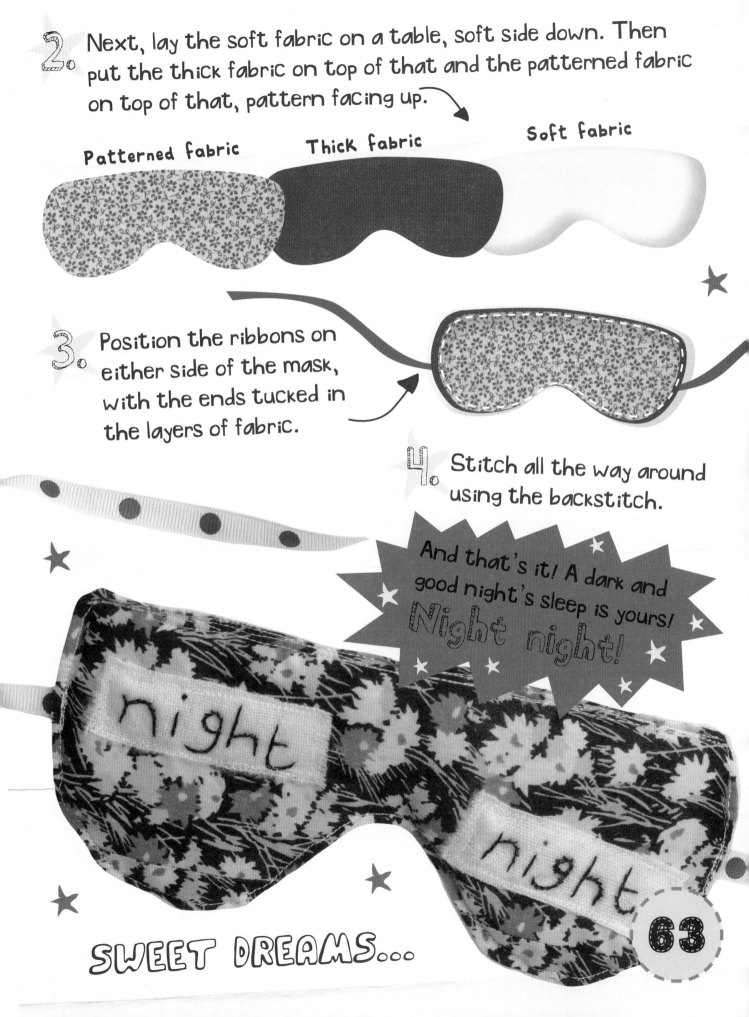

63

CREDITS

Crafts designed and made
by Kate Woods

Photography by
Mike Cooper and
Darren Sawyer.
Photo page
59 courtesy of
iStockphoto.

Illustrations by
Caroline Martin
and
Clare Phillips

Words by
Laura Baker
and
Kate Woods

That was so much fun!